My First Spell Journal

This book belongs to
2iLycAn

 # 2022

JANUARY 2022

S	M	T	W	T	F	S
26	27	28	29	30	31	1
2	3	4	5	6	7	8
9	10	11	12	13	14	15
16	17	18	19	20	21	22
23	24	25	26	27	28	29
30	31					

FEBRUARY 2022

S	M	T	W	T	F	S
30	31	1	2	3	4	5
6	7	8	9	10	11	12
13	14	15	16	17	18	19
20	21	22	23	24	25	26
27	28	1	2	3	4	5

MARCH 2022

S	M	T	W	T	F	S
27	28	1	2	3	4	5
6	7	8	9	10	11	12
13	14	15	16	17	18	19
20	21	22	23	24	25	26
27	28	29	30	31	1	2

APRIL 2022

S	M	T	W	T	F	S
27	28	29	30	31	1	2
3	4	5	6	7	8	9
10	11	12	13	14	15	16
17	18	19	20	21	22	23
24	25	26	27	28	29	30

MAY 2022

S	M	T	W	T	F	S
1	2	3	4	5	6	7
8	9	10	11	12	13	14
15	16	17	18	19	20	21
22	23	24	25	26	27	28
29	30	31	1	2	3	4

JUNE 2022

S	M	T	W	T	F	S
29	30	31	1	2	3	4
5	6	7	8	9	10	11
12	13	14	15	16	17	18
19	20	21	22	23	24	25
26	27	28	29	30	1	2

JULY 2022

S	M	T	W	T	F	S
26	27	28	29	30	1	2
3	4	5	6	7	8	9
10	11	12	13	14	15	16
17	18	19	20	21	22	23
24	25	26	27	28	29	30
31						

AUGUST 2022

S	M	T	W	T	F	S
31	1	2	3	4	5	6
7	8	9	10	11	12	13
14	15	16	17	18	19	20
21	22	23	24	25	26	27
28	29	30	31	1	2	3

SEPTEMBER 2022

S	M	T	W	T	F	S
28	29	30	31	1	2	3
4	5	6	7	8	9	10
11	12	13	14	15	16	17
18	19	20	21	22	23	24
25	26	27	28	29	30	1

OCTOBER 2022

S	M	T	W	T	F	S
25	26	27	28	29	30	1
2	3	4	5	6	7	8
9	10	11	12	13	14	15
16	17	18	19	20	21	22
23	24	25	26	27	28	29
30	31					

NOVEMBER 2022

S	M	T	W	T	F	S
30	31	1	2	3	4	5
6	7	8	9	10	11	12
13	14	15	16	17	18	19
20	21	22	23	24	25	26
27	28	29	30	1	2	3

DECEMBER 2022

S	M	T	W	T	F	S
27	28	29	30	1	2	3
4	5	6	7	8	9	10
11	12	13	14	15	16	17
18	19	20	21	22	23	24
25	26	27	28	29	30	31

BIRTHDAYS

January

Febuary

March

April

May

June

July

August

September

October

November

December

Moon Phases

New Moon

New Beginning

Cleansing & reflecting time, start gathering your thoughts and start planning your goals.

Waxing Moon

A symbol for progression, and a perfect time for goal-setting and achieving. The energy of the waxing moon will help in the process.

Waxing Crescent

Set Intentions

Set your intentions to manifest your wishes.

First Quarter

Take Actions

Get to know your strenght while making actions. Don't give up, even if facing obstacles.

Waxing Gibbous

Alignment

Pay attention to your inner condition and outer surroundings, find your balance and align your vibe with the Universe.

Full Moon

Harvesting

The time to collect the rewards from the actions taken during the previous moons.

Moon Phases

Waning Moon

A symbol for moving inwards, and a perfect time for self-evaluation. Leave the past behind you, and focus on recharging yourself.

Waning Gibbous

Inner Work

Reflect with gratitude on your goals and intentions.

Third Quarter

Letting Go

Let go of all toughts and habits that have negative impact over your life.

Waning Crescent

Relaxing

Relax, reflect, and remain still. Embrace everyting good that comes into your life.

Seasons

SPRING EQUINOX : Often considered the first of the seasons, although there is no set beginning in this never ending cycle. Spring is associated with new beginnings, a time of planning and hopes for the future

CRYSTALS : Carnelian, Agate, Aventurine

SUMMER SOLSTICE : This marks the point where the sun is at its highest. It is associated with good energy and growth.

CRYSTALS : Citrine, Opal, Ruby

AUTUMN EQUINOX : A time of decreased daylight, associated with the harvest and reflection. A time of preparation for winter.

CRYSTALS : Jade, Kyanite, Iron Pyrite

WINTER SOLSTICE : The shortest day of the year, a time of yule and descent into and return of the dark due to the shortest daylight hours.

CRYSTALS : Garnet, Selenite, Amethyst

 # Tides

Spring equinox to summer solstice : The growing tide
Summer solstice to autumn equinox: The reaping tide
Autumn equinox to winter solstice : The resting tide
Winter solstice to spring equinox : The cleansing tide

HERBS

BASIL Magical Properties : Love, exorcism, wealth, sympathy and protection. Dispels confusion, fears & weakness. Drives off hostile spirits. Protects against theft, insanity.

NOTE:
   **Keep a basil leaf in wallet to attract wealth and prosperity.
   **Infuse water with basil and sprinkle over office/shop's door to attract customer
   **Use in peace-making spells after an argument

LAVENDER Magical Properties : Love, clarity sleep, purification, spirituality, dreaming and peace. Promotes healing from depression. Brings peace and harmony.

NOTE :
   **Place dried lavender onto altar to enhance spiritual connection and deepen awareness.
   **Hang lavender onto door to repel negativity and invite peace.
   **Deepen meditations by buring dried lavender as incense.

LEMON BALM Magical Properties : Healing, happiness, cleansing, calming, success, compassion. Use in love charms & spells to attract a partner. Use in healing spells, rituals for anxiety, abuse, low self-esteem.

NOTE :
   **Brew a tea & sip to calm anxiety.
   **Place dried leaves underneath pillow to encourage rejuvinating sleep.
   **Steep leaves in wine and share with partner to strengthen bond.

ROSEMARY Magical Properties : Improve memory. Use for love, loyalty, protection, purification and healing. Prevents nightares and help with unrestful sleep.

NOTE:
   ** Wear or carry while studying, reading or completing tasks to help retain information and aid clear thinking
   ** Burn dried leaves or add to smoke stick to cleanse and purify space.
   ** Plant rosemary outside front door to ward off negativity.

SAGE Magical Properties : Commonly use to smudge and purify and in spells to break unwanted desire. Great for protection, banishing, wishes, wisdom.

NOTE :
   ** Carried to improve mental ability and bring wisdom.
   ** Write on leaves to burn and release desires into the universe.
   ** Use as self-purification and in dealing with grief or loss.

THYME Magical Properties : Protection, courage, strength, bravery, purification, cleansing and open communication with fairies. Ward off nightmares and ensure restful sleep.

NOTE :
   ** Burn and grow in the home for banishing, purification and attract good health, luck and
   ** Wealth as plant grows.
   **Can be used in spells to help keep positive attitude when working on achieving tough goals.

# CRYSTALS

AGATE : Detoxify, strengthen - great for rebalancing the body and eliminate negativity

AMAZONITE : Authenticity, self-love, calming and soothing - helps eliminate fear/ anxiety

AMATHYST: Strong cleansing and healing powers - activates spiritual awareness, protection

AQUAMARINE: Serenity and relaxation, inspiration - powerful crystal to use for meditation

AVENTURINE : Prosperity, opportunity and luck, onnects to earth nature - enhance creativity

BLACK TOURMALINE: Strong grounding energy - protection from negative emotions and intensions

CLEAR QUARTZ: Energizing. Universal healing stone for the mind and body.

DESERT ROSE: Symbolizes all things are possible. Enhances love and teamwork.

FIRE AGATE: The stone of courage, protection, and strength. Enhancing vigor and positive thinking

FLUORIDE: Promotes focus, intuition, and understanding

GREEN AVENTURINE: Promotes positive, easy going attitude towards life

GREEN JADE: Powerful emotional balancer, bringing peace and purity into your life.

HEMATITE: Psychic protection, grounding centering - helps provide courage and strength

JADE: Harmony, prosperity, good luck, friendship - promote wisdom and peace

JASPER POLYCHRONIC: Grounding stone that promotes stability and balancing in life

LABRADORITE: Strengthen aura, divination - banishes fear and insecurity, calms overactive mind

LAPIS LAZULI: Deep self-awareness, inner strength, stone of truth - Encourage truthful speech

LEMURIAN SEED CRYSTAL: Excellent healer used for balancing and clearing chakras.

MALACHITE: Protection, guardian stone - releases negative experiences and old traumas

MOONSTONE: A goddess stone, enhances feminine energies - helps bring about new beginnings

OBSIDIAN : Spiritual protection, strength, grounding - draws out mental stress and tension

ONYX: Alignment, confidence - amplifies intentions, encourage good decision making

PERIDOT: Abundance, positive growth, emotional healing - brings good health happiness

ROSE QUARTZ: Unconditional love, trust, harmony, compassion - helps heal emotional pain

SELENITE: Cleanses aura, helps increase energy, angelic guides - great for meditation

TIGER'S EYE: Helps you stay centered, balance polarities - ideal for building confidence

TURQUOISE: Stone for self-forgiveness, friendship, inner calm - great for depression

TOURMALINE: Black Protects us from external influences, dispersing stress, tension, and negative energy.

CHECK YOUR CRYSTAL'S ENERGY BY HOLDING IT IN YOUR HANDS, CLOSE YOUR EYES AND FEEL THE ITS ENERGY. IF THE FEELING IS TIRED, OR WEAK, RECHARGE IT BY CLEANSING IT WITH WATER, LEAVE IT UNDER THE SUNLIGHT MOONLIGHT, OR WITH OTHER CRYSTALS, SAGE OR SOIL. YOU MAY ALSO CLEANSE IT THE SAME WAY AFTER THE CRYSTAL HAS RESIDUAL ENERGY FROM PAST RITUALS OR NEGATIVE SITUATIONS.

Candles

WHITE
- Spirituality
- Peace
- Higher Self
- Purity
- Substitution

BLACK
- Banishing
- Against
- Negativity
- Protection
- Binding

BRAWN
- Passionate love
- Sexual energy
- Lust
- Physical attraction
- Courage

RED
- Vital Energy
- Strength
- Passion
- Courage,
- Fast Action
- Lust, Charisma

PINK
- Romantic Love
- Emotional
- Healing
- Friendship
- Caring
- Nurturing
- Self-Love

ORANGE
- Business
- Success
- Justice
- Opportunity
- Celebration
- Ambition

YELLOW
- Intelligence
- Learning
- Reason,
- Focus
- Memory,
- Joy,
- Comfort
- Hope

GREEN
- Nature
- Physical
- Healing
- Money
- Abundance
- Fertility
- Growth

PURPLE
- Influence
- Psychic
- Abilities
- Widsom,
- Authority
- Hidden
- Knowledge

SILVER
- Intuition
- Psychism
- Dreams
- Femininity
- The Moon

GOLD
- Wealth
- Masculinity
- Luck, Power
- Happiness
- The Sun

BLUE
- Communication
- Traveling
- Inspiration
- Calm, Creativity
- Forgiveness

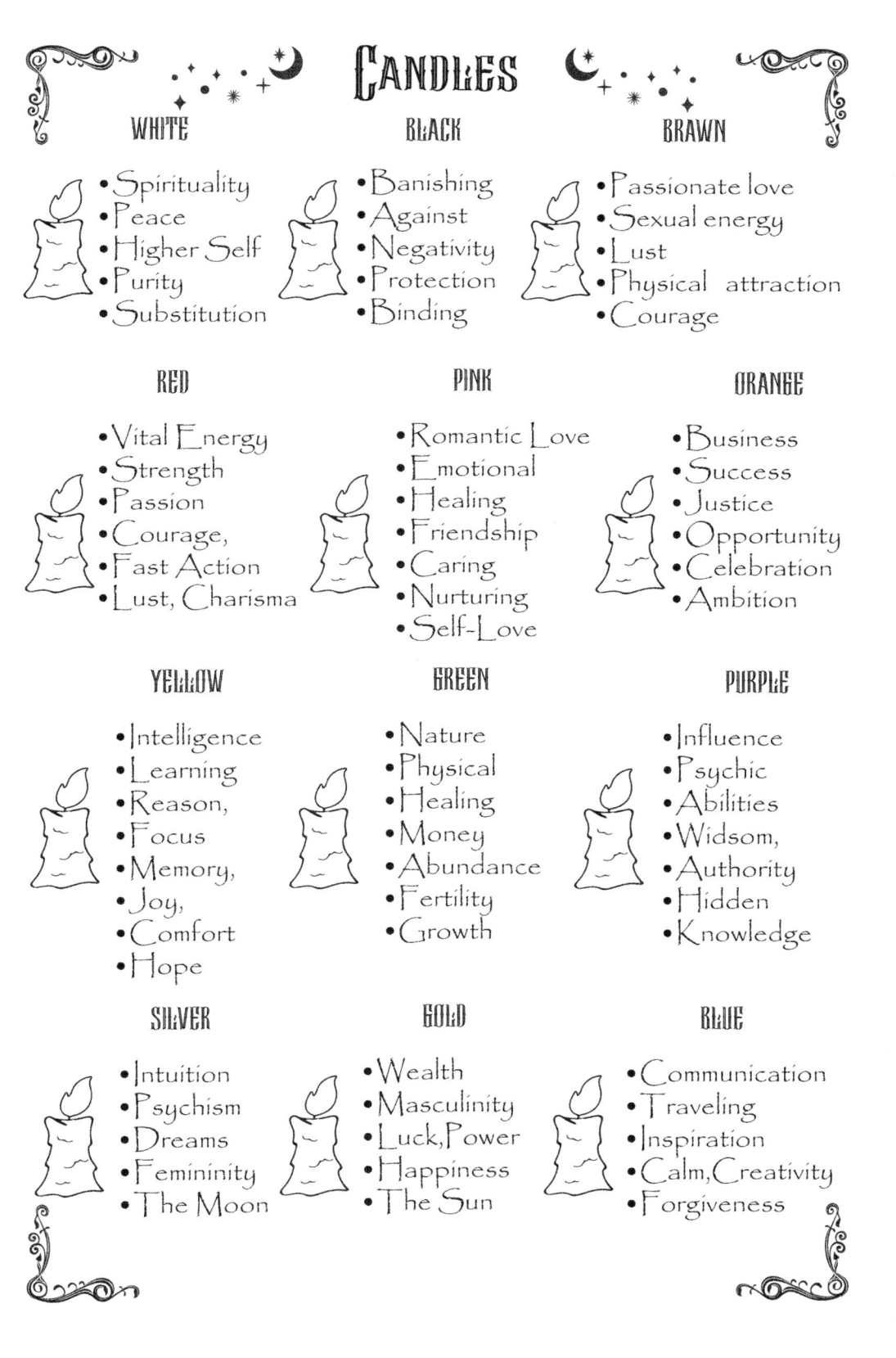

Date _____ Caster _____

Name of Ritual or Spell _____

Intension _____

Moon Phase

Waxing   Fullmoon   Waning

Description	Materials used

Immediate feelings & effects	Participants

Follow up

Manifestation Date _____

Results _____

Notes

Date _____ Caster _____

Name of Ritual or Spell _____

Intension _____

Moon Phase

Waxing   Fullmoon   Waning

Description	Materials used

Immediate feelings & effects	Participants

Follow up

Manifestation Date _____

Results _____

Notes

Date _____ Caster _____

Name of Ritual or Spell _____

Intension _____

Moon Phase

Waxing   Fullmoon   Waning

Description	Materials used

Immediate feelings & effects	Participants

Follow up

Manifestation Date _____

Results _____

Notes

Date _____ Caster _____

Name of Ritual or Spell _____

Intension _____

Moon Phase

Waxing   Fullmoon   Waning

Description	Materials used

Immediate feelings & effects	Participants

Follow up

Manifestation Date _____

Results _____

Notes

Date _____ Caster _____

Name of Ritual or Spell _____

Intension _____

Moon Phase

Waxing   Fullmoon   Waning

Description	Materials used
_____	_____
_____	_____
_____	_____
_____	_____
_____	_____

Immediate feelings & effects	Participants
_____	_____
_____	_____
_____	_____
_____	_____

Follow up

Manifestation Date _____

Results _____

Notes

Date _____ Caster _____

Name of Ritual or Spell _____

Intension _____

Moon Phase

Waxing   Fullmoon   Waning

Description	Materials used
_____	_____
_____	_____
_____	_____
_____	_____
_____	_____

Immediate feelings & effects	Participants
_____	_____
_____	_____
_____	_____
_____	_____

Follow up

Manifestation Date _____

Results _____

Notes

Date_____ Caster_____

Name of Ritual or Spell _____

Intension _____

Moon Phase

Waxing　　　　　Fullmoon　　　　　Waning

Description	Materials used

Immediate feelings & effects	Participants

Follow up

Manifestation Date _____

Results _____

Notes

Date _____ Caster _____

Name of Ritual or Spell _____

Intension _____

Moon Phase

Waxing   Fullmoon   Waning

Description	Materials used

_____
_____
_____
_____
_____

Immediate feelings & effects	Participants

_____
_____
_____
_____

Follow up

Manifestation Date _____

Results _____

Notes

Date_____ Caster_____

Name of Ritual or Spell _____

Intension _____

Moon Phase

Waxing   Fullmoon   Waning

Description	Materials used

Immediate feelings & effects	Participants

Follow up

Manifestation Date _____

Results _____

Notes

Date _____ Caster _____

Name of Ritual or Spell _____

Intension _____

Moon Phase

Waxing   Fullmoon   Waning

Description	Materials used

Immediate feelings & effects	Participants

Follow up

Manifestation Date _____

Results _____

Notes

Date _____ Caster _____

Name of Ritual or Spell _____

Intension _____

Moon Phase

Waxing   Fullmoon   Waning

Description

Materials used

Immediate feelings & effects

Participants

Follow up

Manifestation Date _____

Results _____

Notes

Date _____ Caster _____

Name of Ritual or Spell _____

Intension _____

Moon Phase

Waxing   Fullmoon   Waning

Description	Materials used
_____	_____
_____	_____
_____	_____
_____	_____
_____	_____

Immediate feelings & effects	Participants
_____	_____
_____	_____
_____	_____
_____	_____
_____	_____

Follow up

Manifestation Date _____

Results _____

Notes

Date _____ Caster _____

Name of Ritual or Spell _____

Intension _____

Moon Phase

Waxing   Fullmoon   Waning

Description	Materials used

Immediate feelings & effects	Participants

Follow up

Manifestation Date _____

Results _____

Notes

Date _____ Caster _____

Name of Ritual or Spell _____

Intension _____

Moon Phase

Waxing   Fullmoon   Waning

Description

_____
_____
_____
_____
_____

Materials used

_____
_____
_____
_____
_____

Immediate feelings & effects

_____
_____
_____
_____
_____

Participants

_____
_____
_____
_____
_____

Follow up

Manifestation Date _____

Results _____

Notes

Date _____ Caster _____

Name of Ritual or Spell _____

Intension _____

Moon Phase

Waxing   Fullmoon   Waning

Description	Materials used

_____
_____
_____
_____
_____

Immediate feelings & effects	Participants

_____
_____
_____
_____
_____

Follow up

Manifestation Date _____

Results _____

Date _____ Caster _____

Name of Ritual or Spell _____

Intension _____

Moon Phase

Waxing   Fullmoon   Waning

Description

_____
_____
_____
_____
_____

Materials used

_____
_____
_____
_____
_____

Immediate feelings & effects

_____
_____
_____
_____
_____

Participants

_____
_____
_____
_____
_____

Follow up

Manifestation Date _____

Results _____

Notes

Date _____ Caster _____

Name of Ritual or Spell _____

Intension _____

Moon Phase

Waxing   Fullmoon   Waning

Description	Materials used

Immediate feelings & effects	Participants

Follow up

Manifestation Date _____

Results _____

Notes

Date _____ Caster _____

Name of Ritual or Spell _____

Intension _____

Moon Phase

Waxing   Fullmoon   Waning

Description	Materials used

Immediate feelings & effects	Participants

Follow up

Manifestation Date _____

Results _____

Notes

Date_____ Caster_____

Name of Ritual or Spell _____

Intension _____

Moon Phase

Waxing   Fullmoon   Waning

Description

Materials used

Immediate feelings & effects

Participants

Follow up

Manifestation Date _____

Results _____

Notes

Date _____ Caster _____

Name of Ritual or Spell _____

Intension _____

Moon Phase

Waxing   Fullmoon   Waning

Description

_____
_____
_____
_____
_____

Materials used

_____
_____
_____
_____
_____

Immediate feelings & effects

_____
_____
_____
_____
_____

Participants

_____
_____
_____
_____
_____

Follow up

Manifestation Date _____

Results _____

Notes

Date _____ Caster _____

Name of Ritual or Spell _____

Intension _____

Moon Phase

Waxing   Fullmoon   Waning

Description	Materials used
_____	_____
_____	_____
_____	_____
_____	_____
_____	_____

Immediate feelings & effects	Participants
_____	_____
_____	_____
_____	_____
_____	_____
_____	_____

Follow up

Manifestation Date _____

Results _____

Notes

Date _____ Caster _____

Name of Ritual or Spell _____

Intension _____

Moon Phase

Waxing   Fullmoon   Waning

Description	Materials used

_____   _____

_____   _____

_____   _____

_____   _____

_____   _____

Immediate feelings & effects	Participants

_____   _____

_____   _____

_____   _____

_____   _____

_____   _____

Follow up

Manifestation Date _____

Results _____

Notes

Date _____ Caster _____

Name of Ritual or Spell _____

Intension _____

Moon Phase

Waxing   Fullmoon   Waning

Description	Materials used

Immediate feelings & effects	Participants

Follow up

Manifestation Date _____

Results _____

Notes

Date _____ Caster _____

Name of Ritual or Spell _____

Intension _____

Moon Phase

Waxing   Fullmoon   Waning

Description	Materials used

Immediate feelings & effects	Participants

Follow up

Manifestation Date _____

Results _____

Notes

Date _____ Caster _____

Name of Ritual or Spell _____

Intension _____

Moon Phase

Waxing   Fullmoon   Waning

Description	Materials used

_____   _____

_____   _____

_____   _____

_____   _____

_____   _____

Immediate feelings & effects	Participants

_____   _____

_____   _____

_____   _____

_____   _____

_____   _____

Follow up

Manifestation Date _____

Results _____

Notes

Date _____ Caster _____

Name of Ritual or Spell _____

Intension _____

Moon Phase

Waxing   Fullmoon   Waning

Description

_____
_____
_____
_____
_____

Materials used

_____
_____
_____
_____
_____

Immediate feelings & effects

_____
_____
_____
_____
_____

Participants

_____
_____
_____
_____
_____

Follow up

Manifestation Date _____

Results _____

Notes

Date _____ Caster _____

Name of Ritual or Spell _____

Intension _____

Moon Phase

Waxing   Fullmoon   Waning

Description	Materials used

Immediate feelings & effects	Participants

Follow up

Manifestation Date _____

Results _____

Notes

Date _____ Caster _____

Name of Ritual or Spell _____

Intension _____

Moon Phase

Waxing   Fullmoon   Waning

Description	Materials used

_____

Immediate feelings & effects | Participants

_____

Follow up

Manifestation Date _____

Results _____

Notes

Date _____ Caster _____

Name of Ritual or Spell _____

Intension _____

Moon Phase

Waxing   Fullmoon   Waning

Description	Materials used

_____

Immediate feelings & effects	Participants

_____

Follow up

Manifestation Date _____

Results _____

Notes

Date _____ Caster _____

Name of Ritual or Spell _____

Intension _____

Moon Phase

Waxing   Fullmoon   Waning

Description	Materials used
_____	_____
_____	_____
_____	_____
_____	_____
_____	_____

Immediate feelings & effects	Participants
_____	_____
_____	_____
_____	_____
_____	_____

Follow up

Manifestation Date _____

Results _____

Notes

Date _____ Caster _____

Name of Ritual or Spell _____

Intension _____

Moon Phase

Waxing   Fullmoon   Waning

Description

_____
_____
_____
_____
_____

Materials used

_____
_____
_____
_____

Immediate feelings & effects

_____
_____
_____
_____
_____

Participants

_____
_____
_____
_____

Follow up

Manifestation Date _____

Results _____

Notes

Date _____ Caster _____

Name of Ritual or Spell _____

Intension _____

Moon Phase

Waxing   Fullmoon   Waning

Description	Materials used

_____

Immediate feelings & effects	Participants

_____

Follow up

Manifestation Date _____

Results _____

Notes

Date_____ Caster_____

Name of Ritual or Spell _____

Intension _____

Moon Phase

Waxing   Fullmoon   Waning

Description	Materials used

Immediate feelings & effects	Participants

Follow up

Manifestation Date _____

Results _____

Notes

Date _____ Caster _____

Name of Ritual or Spell _____

Intension _____

Moon Phase

Waxing   Fullmoon   Waning

Description	Materials used

Immediate feelings & effects	Participants

Follow up

Manifestation Date _____

Results _____

Notes

Date _____ Caster _____

Name of Ritual or Spell _____

Intension _____

Moon Phase

Waxing   Fullmoon   Waning

Description	Materials used
_____	_____
_____	_____
_____	_____
_____	_____
_____	_____

Immediate feelings & effects	Participants
_____	_____
_____	_____
_____	_____
_____	_____
_____	_____

Follow up

Manifestation Date _____

Results _____

Notes

Date _____ Caster _____

Name of Ritual or Spell _____

Intension _____

Moon Phase

Waxing   Fullmoon   Waning

Description	Materials used

Immediate feelings & effects	Participants

Follow up

Manifestation Date _____

Results _____

Notes

Date _____ Caster _____

Name of Ritual or Spell _____

Intension _____

Moon Phase

Waxing   Fullmoon   Waning

Description	Materials used
_____	_____
_____	_____
_____	_____
_____	_____
_____	_____

Immediate feelings & effects	Participants
_____	_____
_____	_____
_____	_____
_____	_____
_____	_____

Follow up

Manifestation Date _____

Results _____

Notes

Date _____ Caster _____

Name of Ritual or Spell _____

Intension _____

Moon Phase

Waxing   Fullmoon   Waning

Description	Materials used

Immediate feelings & effects	Participants

Follow up

Manifestation Date _____

Results _____

Notes

Date _____ Caster _____

Name of Ritual or Spell _____

Intension _____

Moon Phase

Waxing   Fullmoon   Waning

Description

_____
_____
_____
_____
_____

Materials used

_____
_____
_____
_____
_____

Immediate feelings & effects

_____
_____
_____
_____
_____

Participants

_____
_____
_____
_____
_____

Follow up

Manifestation Date _____

Results _____

Notes

Date _____ Caster _____

Name of Ritual or Spell _____

Intension _____

Moon Phase

Waxing   Fullmoon   Waning

Description

Materials used

Immediate feelings & effects

Participants

Follow up

Manifestation Date _____

Results _____

Notes

Date _____ Caster _____

Name of Ritual or Spell _____

Intension _____

Moon Phase

Waxing   Fullmoon   Waning

Description	Materials used

Immediate feelings & effects	Participants

Follow up

Manifestation Date _____

Results _____

Notes

Date _____ Caster_____

Name of Ritual or Spell _____

Intension _____

Moon Phase

Waxing   Fullmoon   Waning

Description

_____
_____
_____
_____
_____

Materials used

_____
_____
_____
_____
_____

Immediate feelings & effects

_____
_____
_____
_____
_____

Participants

_____
_____
_____
_____
_____

Follow up

Manifestation Date _____

Results _____

Notes

Date _____ Caster _____

Name of Ritual or Spell _____

Intension _____

Moon Phase

Waxing   Fullmoon   Waning

Description	Materials used

Immediate feelings & effects	Participants

Follow up

Manifestation Date _____

Results _____

Notes

Date _____ Caster _____

Name of Ritual or Spell _____

Intension _____

Moon Phase

Waxing   Fullmoon   Waning

Description	Materials used

Immediate feelings & effects	Participants

❧ Follow up ❧

Manifestation Date _____

Results _____

Notes

Date _____ Caster _____

Name of Ritual or Spell _____

Intension _____

Moon Phase

Waxing   Fullmoon   Waning

Description	Materials used

Immediate feelings & effects	Participants

Follow up

Manifestation Date _____

Results _____

Notes

Date _____ Caster _____

Name of Ritual or Spell _____

Intension _____

Moon Phase

Waxing   Fullmoon   Waning

Description

_____
_____
_____
_____

Materials used

_____
_____
_____
_____

Immediate feelings & effects

_____
_____
_____
_____

Participants

_____
_____
_____
_____

Follow up

Manifestation Date _____

Results _____

Notes

Date _____ Caster _____

Name of Ritual or Spell _____

Intension _____

Moon Phase

Waxing   Fullmoon   Waning

Description	Materials used

Immediate feelings & effects	Participants

Follow up

Manifestation Date _____

Results _____

Notes

Date_____ Caster_____

Name of Ritual or Spell _____

Intension _____

Moon Phase

Waxing   Fullmoon   Waning

Description

Materials used

Immediate feelings & effects

Participants

Follow up

Manifestation Date _____

Results _____

Notes

Date_____ Caster_____

Name of Ritual or Spell _____

Intension _____

Moon Phase

Waxing   Fullmoon   Waning

Description

_____
_____
_____
_____
_____
_____

Materials used

_____
_____
_____
_____

Immediate feelings & effects

_____
_____
_____
_____
_____

Participants

_____
_____
_____
_____
_____

Follow up

Manifestation Date _____

Results _____

Notes

Date_____ Caster_____

Name of Ritual or Spell _____

Intension _____

Moon Phase

Waxing   Fullmoon   Waning

Description

_____
_____
_____
_____

Materials used

_____
_____
_____

Immediate feelings & effects

_____
_____
_____
_____

Participants

_____
_____
_____

Follow up

Manifestation Date _____

Results _____

Notes

Thank you

Printed in Great Britain
by Amazon